Famous Ships of the Twentieth Century

by Claire Daniel

Harcourt

SCHOOL PUBLISHERS

ISBN 10: 0-15-350594-X
ISBN 13: 978-0-15-350594-2

Ordering Options
ISBN 10: 0-15-350336-X (Grade 6 Below-Level Collection)
ISBN 13: 978-0-15-350336-8 (Grade 6 Below-Level Collection)
ISBN 10: 0-15-357739-8 (package of 5)
ISBN 13: 978-0-15-357739-0 (package of 5)

4 5 6 7 8 9 10   0940   12 11 10 09

Many ships have been lost at sea, and each has its own story. Icebergs, torpedoes, mines, and fog can become deadly weapons to a large ship. Some ships have disappeared mysteriously, leaving people wondering what really happened to them.

Between the years 1900 and 2000, countless ships were shipwrecked. Among them are some of the more famous doomed ships, including the *Titanic*, the *Morro Castle*, the *U.S.S. Cyclops*, the *Empress of Ireland*, and the *Brittanic*.

The *Titanic*

Perhaps the most famous of all shipwrecks is the *Titanic*. The ship set sail on April 10, 1912, on its maiden voyage from England. Five days later, it hit an iceberg and sank to the bottom of the Atlantic Ocean.

People had believed that the *Titanic* was unsinkable because the builders had included new safety features. These features included watertight compartments that would seal if the ship was taking on water. The ship was thought to be so safe that the British Board of Trade, which determined how many lifeboats were required, said that it was unnecessary to have enough lifeboats for all the passengers.

When the *Titanic* hit the iceberg, people didn't panic at first. Passengers and crew didn't think the iceberg had done much damage. Only when the ship began to tilt did people begin to panic. Only two and a half hours after the ship hit the iceberg, the *Titanic* sank, and more than 1,500 lives were lost.

Many explorers have examined the shipwreck in the past twenty years, and they have come to an interesting conclusion. The ship did not sink because the iceberg ripped a hole in the ship's side. Instead, the iceberg caused the metal bolts that held the ship together to pop open. This caused the metal plates of the ship to separate. That was probably why the huge ship sank.

The *Morro Castle*

The *Morro Castle* was a ship built to carry passengers in style. Its lavish rooms were made to comfortably carry 437 first-class passengers and 95 in the more modest accommodations of tourist class. The last voyage of the *Morro Castle* went from Havana, Cuba (located in the Caribbean, south of Florida), to New York City.

Events that occurred before the sinking of the *Morro Castle* on September 9, 1935, were curious. Its captain, Robert Wilmott, had died as he was taking a bath that evening. First Officer William Warms took over command, but hours later, at 2:45 A.M., a fire broke out in the first-class section of the ship.

From then on, Warms made a series of bad judgments. First, he turned the ship in a direction that actually fanned the fire. He also failed to send out an SOS, or a call for help.

Thick smoke made it difficult for people to find their way to safety. People panicked, and the lifeboats actually left carrying only some of the crew and just a handful of passengers. The people left behind jumped overboard, and some were picked up by other ships.

One hundred thirty-seven passengers and crew died in all. The remains of the burning ship washed ashore, but to this day, no one knows how the fire started. Arson, when someone sets a fire on purpose, was suspected.

The *U.S.S. Cyclops*

The *U.S.S. Cyclops* was filled with huge quantities of manganese ore (an essential element used to make steel) as it traveled from Barbados (located in the Caribbean Sea) to Baltimore, Maryland. The time was March 1918, and World War I was coming to an end.

The *Cyclops* disappeared mysteriously, and no trace of her has ever been found. We do know that shortly before she disappeared, there was a minor mutiny by the crew, when the crew tried to rebel against the captain. The captain took control, and the offenders were sent below deck in irons.

That is all that is known because the ship was never heard from or seen again. There is no evidence that any enemy submarines sank the ship. People have many theories about its disappearance. Some even believe that a giant sea monster grabbed the ship and pulled it to the bottom of the ocean. Others believe a sudden storm sank the ship. Still, another theory comes from the fact that the *Cyclops* disappeared in the Bermuda Triangle.

The Bermuda Triangle is an area between Florida, Bermuda, and Puerto Rico. During the last hundred years, more than fifty ships and twenty airplanes have disappeared from this area without leaving a trace. Some think that strange forces cause the ships and airplanes to disappear although nothing has ever been proven.

The *Empress of Ireland*

At 2:00 A.M., on May 29, 1914, the *Empress of Ireland* was moving slowly down the St. Lawrence River (located in eastern Canada). This was two years after the sinking of the *Titanic*. The *Empress of Ireland* was not a lavish ship like the *Titanic*, but she was carrying almost as many passengers and crew—some 1,477 people.

Fog would be the ship's enemy that early morning. Captain Henry Kendall spotted a ship about eight miles (13 km) away. The ship was coming towards the *Empress*, but he figured that he had time to cross her path before reaching open water. The ships came closer and closer, safely apart.

However, a thick fog crept in and soon swallowed up both ships. The approaching ship, the *Storstad*, thought that the *Empress* was passing them on the port (left) side. The *Empress* thought the *Storstad* was passing them on the starboard (right) side.

Both were wrong. Suddenly, Captain Kendall saw a dreaded sight. The *Storstad* was coming through the murky fog, headed straight toward his ship! The bow (front) of the *Storstad* tore through the body of the *Empress of Ireland*, and the *Empress* sank fourteen minutes later. Many of the people aboard were sleeping. 1,012 people lost their lives. The *Storstad* was badly damaged but did not sink.

The *Britannic*

The *Britannic* was the sister ship of the *Titanic*. After the *Titanic* disaster, its builders were determined to make a truly unsinkable ship, so they had designed it to be even safer. This included an inner skin that would further protect the ship from ever sinking.

The builders had made the ship the most lavish ever, but it was never to become a passenger ship. Instead, war had claimed her services. The *Britannic* became a British hospital ship during World War I. Instead of fancy trimmings, the decks were filled with hospital beds. The dining room became an intensive care ward.

According to international laws, the *Britannic* was protected from submarine attack. A hospital ship could not be attacked or torpedoed. Still, it was wartime, and the captain was cautious of dangerous German submarines. On its sixth voyage, the medical staff was traveling from England to hospitals in Egypt, India, and Malta to pick up and treat soldiers wounded from the war.

The *Britannic* was sailing near Greece when it met its fate. Unsinkable or not, an explosion caused it to sink. Some people onboard said they saw a torpedo, but there were no German submarines in the area. Others believe that the ship ran into a mine, a bomb planted in the ocean by the German navy. The ship sank in fifty-five minutes and became the largest sunken ocean liner in the world.

The launching of the *Britannic*

In 1995, Robert Ballard explored the wreck off the coast of the Greek island of Kea in the Aegean Sea to find out why the ship sank. After Ballard's ascent from where the *Britannic* lay, he reported his findings. He could not find evidence of a mine explosion, but he couldn't prove that the ship had sunk because of a torpedo either. The reason for the ship's fateful explosion is still a mystery.

Today people continue to sail on the sea. After reading about all these shipwrecks, you might think that it happens often. However, over the years, there have relatively been few shipwrecks.

The small port of Korissia on the Greek island, Kea.

Think Critically

1. Why do you think that it is important for passengers not to panic when a ship is sinking?

2. Compare and contrast the two ships, the *Britannic* and the *Titanic*.

3. How does fog make it dangerous for passing ships?

4. Would you recommend this book to a friend? Why or why not?

5. What was the most interesting fact you learned about shipwrecks?

 Science

Bermuda Triangle Do research on the Internet or use other library resources to learn about the Bermuda Triangle. What do scientists know about the area that might explain why so many boats and planes have disappeared? Write several paragraphs explaining your finding.

 **School-Home Connection** Ask a family member whether they know about any shipwrecks. Then share what you have learned.